TERROR U

by Clare Oliver

Contents

AT THE SHORELINE

The beach is the place where the land meets the sea and monsters of the deep can come ashore. Dolphins and killer whales may look cute, but these warm-blooded mammals are cool killers!

Killer whale

BIG AND SCARY

Killer whales are huge. Their dorsal (back) fin alone is as tall as a man! These fierce hunters are aggressive enough to go for prey much bigger than themselves, including humpback whales.

Bottlenose dolphin

DOLPHIN BULLIES

Not all whales and dolphins have teeth but most need them to tear at their meals of fish and seals. Male dolphins also use theirs to show other dolphins who's boss. By biting or snapping their jaws they scare off rival mates— and give them some horrible scars.

SINISTER SURFERS

In Antarctic waters off the coast of Patagonia, the killer whale practices a very sinister kind of surfing. It waits for a really big wave and rides it to shore—straight into a group of unsuspecting sea lion pups. The hunter snaps a squealing pup in its mouth, just in time for the next wave to carry it back out to sea. Split-second timing saves the whale from being beached.

PLAYING WITH DINNER

Death is not instant for the baby sea lion. First the killer whale plays "catch," tossing its victim into the air and batting it with its tail. But before long, hunger takes over: the whale gulps down its prey in a single swallow.

SEA QUIZ

How many types of whale and dolphin do killer whales attack?
a) 10
b) 15
c) 25

How fast can a killer whale swim?

a) 22 mph
b) 34.5 mph
c) 70.5 mph

How many teeth does a long-snouted spinner dolphin have?

a) up to 92
b) 92-171
c) 172-252

(answers on page 32)

BREATHING APPARATUS

Killer whales and dolphins are air-breathing mammals like us. They must come up to the surface for air.

KILLING MACHINE

Once a shark knows you're there, you're in trouble! Hidden inside the shark's huge skull are two inner ears. The shark can hear the splashing of a likely victim from about 275 yards away (that's about the length of five Olympic swimming pools).

BUILT TO BEND

Instead of bones, sharks have skeletons made of cartilage. That's the same bendy stuff that you have in your ears and nose. This makes the shark's spine super-flexible and allows it to twist and turn in the water as it chases its prey.

GREEDY GUTS

Tiger sharks will gulp down almost anything. Items found inside their stomachs include a goat, ships' anchors, license plates, whole suits of armor, tires and, of course, human beings!

Dorsal fin *This is the scary back fin which tells a swimmer that danger is coming! The shark uses this fin to keep its body balanced and level in the water.*

Tail fin *This fin gives the shark great speed. By swishing the tail from side to side, the shark propels itself through the water.*

Blue shark

SEA QUIZ

Which of these fish is not a shark?

a) whale shark
b) dogfish
c) megamouth

How long does an adult shark's set of teeth last?

a) about a week
b) a month or two
c) about a year

How many times faster than an Olympic swimmer is a tiger shark?

a) twice
b) three times
c) six times

(answers on page 32)

COLD-BLOODED KILLERS

Most sharks are cold-blooded, so their bodies stay at the same temperature as the water around them. Not so with the speed champions, such as the mako or the great white. These sharks keep their blood temperature higher than the water they swim in, which means their muscles are warm too. Warm muscles can work harder: the great white has double the power of a cold-blooded shark.

TOOTHSOME TALES

Most sharks get through hundreds of pairs of teeth in a lifetime. The mako's teeth are the scariest looking of all: long daggers that hold prey in a death grip.

Mako shark's teeth

Pectoral fins

The flow of water over these front fins gives the shark lift in the water, rather like a plane's wings give it lift in the air. Pectoral fins also help the shark to steer its course.

SHARK ATTACK

The ocean creature that gets the worst press is the shark. This lean, mean killing machine is designed to do damage and the meanest of all is the great white, or "man-eater" shark. Sleek and streamlined, it can shoot through the water at speeds of up to 18 mph.

Great white shark

SNIFFING OUT A MEAL

After the man-eater shark has sounded you out, it changes course and swims straight for you. It moves its head from side to side so that water flows into each nostril. This allows the shark to work out where your scent is strongest.

FANG MONSTER

The prehistoric megalodon shark had teeth that were 6 inches long—that's a fang four times longer than the great white's.

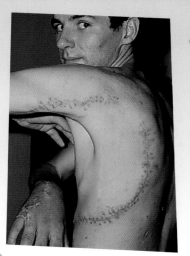

CLEAN CUT

The shark's teeth are so sharp that survivors of attacks say you don't even feel the bite. Unfortunately, few of those attacked live to tell the tale. This fisherman was lucky, but the toothy scars from the hungry great white that attacked him are permanent.

A SPECIAL SENSE

Just before the shark bites, pores on its snout pick up tiny electrical signals from your heart and muscles. Thanks to these supersensitive pores, called *ampullae of Lorennzini*, the mean man-eater knows exactly when and where to snap shut its ginormous jaws.

MAN-EATERS

There are about 250 different species of shark, but most feed on large fish and seals—not human beings! The ones with a taste for your blood are great whites, tiger sharks, blue sharks, makos, and black-tip sharks.

SEA QUIZ

How wide can a great white open its jaws?
a) less than 1 yard
b) more than 1 yard
c) more than 2 yards

How many people are killed by sharks in a year?
a) 20-30
b) 30-100
c) 100-200

How many species of shark have attacked people?
a) 40
b) 125
c) 250

(answers on page 32)

FEEDING FRENZY

Bluefish hunt in packs that are thousands strong. Together, these killers work themselves up into a feeding frenzy, attacking anything in their way as they cruise through the water. They only have time to snap at their food, leaving behind a trail of blood and lots of half-eaten, dying fish.

School of bluefish

SEA QUIZ

How long is a bluefish?

a) 47 inches
b) 100 inches
c) 180 inches

Which of these is not another name for a bluefish?

a) shoaler
b) tailor
c) snapper

How many dorsal fins do barracudas and bluefish have?

a) one
b) two
c) three

(answers on page 32)

PREDATOR ALERT!

All barracuda are predators, but most feed on small fish such as anchovies or mullets. These fearless fish are well-known for their curiosity and, of course, for their huge, sharp teeth. The great barracuda has occasionally been known to attack humans swimming in warm, tropical seas.

LONG & LEAN

It's not surprising the savage barracuda has such an appetite. At over 6 feet long, it could fit you in its stomach with room to spare.

KILLER GANGS

When fierce hunters join forces to form monster gangs, the results can be devastating. Barracuda and bluefish are the piranhas of the seas, with teeth to match. They can wipe out a school of fish in minutes.

SHOALING SHARKS

Not all sharks hunt solo like the great white. Grey nurse sharks group together in gangs. Together, they use wolf-like tactics to herd unsuspecting dogfish, squid, or lobsters. Once the prey is surrounded, all the sharks can settle down to enjoy the feast.

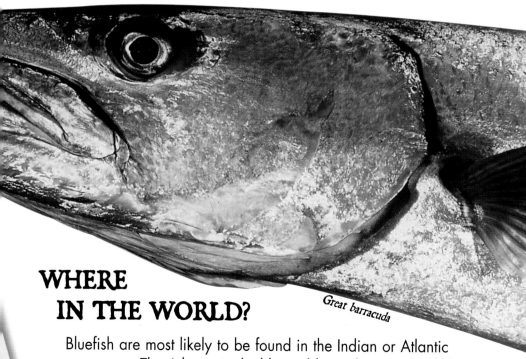

Great barracuda

WHERE IN THE WORLD?

Bluefish are most likely to be found in the Indian or Atlantic oceans. The Atlantic is double-trouble, as barracudas lurk there too, as well as in the Caribbean and western Pacific.

HARMLESS GIANTS

Not all of the monsters of the deep are out to get us! Some of the biggest, scariest-looking fish and sea mammals are completely harmless. Unless you happen to be microscopic plankton or krill, that is!

WHAT A WHOPPER!

The whale shark may be the world's biggest fish, but it shares the oceans with an even bigger creature—the blue whale. At about 80 feet long and weighing over 100 tons, this record-breaking mammal is the biggest creature on the planet.

SHARK PARTY

Whale sharks often form shoals and swim the seas together. Cruising whale sharks like to take it slow and that's when they spell trouble for us humans: sometimes boats have capsized after colliding with them!

Whale shark

SEA QUIZ

How long is a whale shark?

a) 16 feet
b) 33 feet
c) 59 feet

What's the record for the longest blue whale?

a) 88.5 feet
b) 98.5 feet
c) 108.2 feet

How long can a blue whale stay under water?

a) 45 minutes
b) 1 hour
c) 2 hours

(answers on page 32)

GENTLE GIANT

The whale shark is not nearly as scary as its man-eating cousins. It may be enormous, but this harmless shark is happy to feed on some of the smallest things in the sea—miniature plants and animals called plankton. Inside its gaping mouth are over 300 bands of tiny teeth which the shark uses to crunch up its dinner.

Whale shark

The whale shark is the world's biggest fish. It weighs as much as six elephants!

COLANDER MOUTH

Like the whale shark, the blue whale feeds on tiny creatures called krill. In a single gulp, the whale takes in about 6 cubic yards of water. In one hour, that adds up to enough water to fill a swimming pool. The giant whale doesn't have any teeth but it uses special plates in its mouth called baleen to sieve out the tiny animals.

SLIPPERY SERPENTS

Snakes are scary enough on land, but did you know there are snakes in the ocean, too? There are over 50 different species of sea snake, all found in tropical waters off the coasts of Australia and Asia, where the temperature is high enough to warm their cold-blooded bodies.

WRITHING WRIGGLERS

Most sea snakes live on coral reefs or in coastal mangrove swamps. Sometimes, they join together to form a huge wriggling mass. This writhing raft floats on the surface, basking in the warm rays of the sun.

Olive sea snake

SERPENT'S KISS

Like many land snakes, sea snakes have a venomous bite. Luckily, sea snakes only bite for two reasons: either in self-defense, or because they want to paralyze their prey (which includes creatures such as eels and fish). The venom is pumped into the victim from glands in their two fangs, just like a cobra's. Watch out if you see a Belcher's sea snake, though. Its venom is 100 times more powerful than any other snake's.

The oarfish is the longest fish in the sea—so far as we know! It's as long as four canoes placed end-to-end.

THAT'S OAR-FULLY LONG!

FREAKY FISH

The most likely candidate for being a sea serpent is not a snake at all. The handsome oarfish usually lives in deep tropical waters, so few get to admire its long, silvery body and majestic red crest. Oarfish grow to a length of 30 feet, but in 1963, scientists spotted one swimming off New Jersey that was a whopping 50 feet long!

New Caledonian sea snake

DOING THE CONGA

The biggest ever sea-snake party happened in 1932 in the Strait of Malacca, off Malaysia. The massed millions of *Astrotia stokesii* sea snakes formed a line that was 10 feet wide and 62 miles long!

SEA QUIZ

Which other reptile is at home in the open sea?
a) saltwater croc
b) garter snake
c) Galapagos tortoise

From which part of their body do sea snakes get rid of excess salt?

a) their bottom
b) their tongue
c) their ears

Which sea snake goes right out to sea?

a) olive sea snake
b) Hardwicke's sea snake
c) pelagic sea snake

(answers on page 32)

BIG SOFTIES

Who'd hang out with a predator? Strangely, lots of little creatures do seem to form friendships with underwater nasties and some even climb into their mouths! By helping out someone bigger than themselves, they usually get something in return, even if it's just protection from other scary beasts.

Hermit crab

SEA QUIZ

Who snacks on an ocean sunfish's lice?

a) great white
b) gulper eel
c) herring gull

Which fish makes its home in an anemone?

a) Atlantic cod
b) clownfish
c) catfish

Where is the world's biggest coral reef?

a) off Australia
b) off France
c) off Argentina

(answers on page 32)

DEADLY DEFENCE

The hermit crab finds the poisonous anemone so useful in keeping crab-eating predators away, that it remembers its friend when it moves into a bigger house. With a perfect pincer movement, the crab gently transfers the anemone from its old shell to its new one.

CRAFTY CRAB

One crab that lives in the Indian Ocean goes one further. It carries around two anemones, one on the end of each front claw. If any predator dares to approach, the anemones' stinging tentacles pack a painful punch!

WHY SHELL OUT FOR A HOUSE?

Hermit crabs are well known for making their home in other creatures' shells. But some move into a different kind of shell—a coconut!

Sea anemone

VALET SERVICE

Groupers are predators who live in coral reefs. Every day or so, when they are in need of a cleaning, they visit a particular place on the reef to be "serviced." At the cleaning station, a troupe of shrimp or tiny fish called cleaner wrasses set to work. These creatures crawl all over the grouper, removing lice and dead skin, picking off any fungus and even cleaning the grouper's teeth!

The shrimp are very hard-working, sometimes sprucing up to 50 groupers every hour. The groupers leave feeling spic and span—and the shrimp have had a free meal. *Coral grouper and shrimp*

STONE DEAD

The stonefish is the most poisonous fish in the sea. It looks just like a lump of rock, but it's far more deadly. If you were to accidentally tread on one, you could soon be stone dead. Spiny needles on the stonefish's fins inject a strong poison that makes you crazy—some victims have been known to bite anyone trying to help them.

Stonefish

Stargazer

SANDY HIDE-OUT

The stargazer gets its name because its eyes are on the top of its head, but this isn't so the fish can look at the stars and dream. It's so that it can bury itself in the sand and hide, keeping an eye out for passing prey. While it waits, the stargazer remains completely still, but once a suitable meal swims past, the fish rises up as if from nowhere—and snatches it!

UNDERWATER SCORPION

Scorpion fish

The scorpion fish looks more like seaweed than a land scorpion—and it's supposed to. Frondy fins and way-out patterning help the fish to blend in with its background of coral reef weeds. Its mouth is partly see-through, making it even more likely that prey will accidentally swim right in—to their deaths.

HIDDEN HORROR

Lurking on the sea bed are some deadly hunters.
Worst of all, their cunning camouflage makes
them invisible, until it's too late...

LEAF ME ALONE!

Some sea creatures use camouflage as defense, not to attack. The cockatoo waspfish's body looks just like a dead leaf, and the fish even plays dead to let the current rock it back and forth as if it were a leaf. As extra armor, the waspfish has venomous spines on its dorsal fin.

CLOWN COSTUME

The clownfish's coloring makes clever camouflage against the bright corals of the reef. Just right for avoiding predators—most of the time.

SEA QUIZ

How many types of stonefish are there?

a) 1
b) 10
c) 20

How many poisonous spines does the Indian stonefish have?

a) 13—unlucky for some!
b) 7
c) 3

How long is a stargazer?

a) 3.9 inches
b) 19.6 inches
c) 39.3 inches

(answers on page 32)

DEEP WATER

Below 13,000 feet, the ocean is dark and cold. No sunlight filters down. Here in the abyss live some of the strangest-looking fish of all. Most have huge, gaping jaws and ugly, staring eyes, yet these ghoulish creatures are usually no bigger than your ruler, because food is much more scarce in the abyss.

SEA QUIZ

How many species of deep-sea anglerfish are there?
a) 3
b) 40
c) 100

What doesn't an anglerfish have?
a) scales
b) gills
c) sight

A female dragonfish is 11.8 inches — how long is her mate?
a) 1.9 inches
b) 11.8 inches
c) 19.6 inches

(answers on page 32)

FEROCIOUS FANGS

The fangtooth is a deep-sea oddball with grotesque teeth. Cruising at depths of about 2,000 feet, it picks up squid and other tasty snacks. At 6,500 feet, it homes in on dragonfish and other fangy prey.

Fangtooth fish

GONE FISHING

Anglerfish live anywhere where they can find food. These underwater weirdos have to be one of the strangest fish of all. Their bulgy bodies don't need to be streamlined, because the best way to catch their meal is to keep still. Curved teeth create a cage to trap unsuspecting creatures that have swum too close.

VICIOUS VIPER

At 11.8 inches long, the viperfish is big for a deep-sea fish. In the gloomy depths, it has come up with a clever way to attract its prey. Dangling from its dorsal fin is a glow-in-the-dark lure. This works like the maggot on the end of a fisherman's line, but any fish that's tempted meets with the viperfish's terrifying jaws, not a juicy worm. These grip the prey with a vice-like hold.

Viperfish

FLIPPING OUT

The stomiatoid has a neat trick for gulping down a big dinner. Its whole head flips back so that it can swallow prey as wide as its own head!

19

LEG GO!

If a predator bites off the ray (arm) of a starfish, the starfish simply grows a new one!

OUCH!

Lionfish

STING SOLDIER

The Portuguese man-of-war jellyfish floats on the surface of warm seas. Its see-through body is shaded a delicate pink or blue. Sometimes, thousands of the jellyfish congregate together—and they are best avoided. Stinging cells called neatocysts on their tentacles deliver a nasty sting, which is strong enough to send you into shock and can affect your heartbeat or breathing.

Giant pelagic jellyfish

JELLY HEAD

In 1998 a new species of giant jellyfish was found in the eastern Pacific. Scientists named it *Chrysaora achlyos*. This rubbery monster has a 39 inch wide purply-black bell and its pale pink tentacles trail 19 feet behind. Scientists still don't know how powerful its sting is–and no one has volunteered to find out!

If you've ever been stung by a jellyfish, you know about it. All sorts of sea creatures give vicious stings, either to stun prey or ward off an attacker. When a human being is the victim, there is usually an antidote, but sometimes the result is death.

PRICKLY PORCUPINE

The lionfish is named for its frilly mane. This is far from soft— it's made up of spines like a porcupine's quills. On the tip of each hollow spine is deadly poison, which would give a hungry shark a very nasty surprise.

SPIKES AND SPINES

Sea urchins like to be left alone to gnaw algae off the rocks or nibble on other favourite foods. And thanks to their poisonous prickles, few predators attack them. The hatpin urchin's spines are scarily big at 12 inches long—and probably a bit too large for a hat! The slate-pencil urchin's spines are much shorter but they are so thick they can be used to write with.

SEA QUIZ

How long were the longest-ever jellyfish tentacles?

a) 34.4 feet
b) 57.4 feet
c) 11.8 feet

Which jellyfish's sting can kill you in minutes?

a) raspberry jellyfish
b) sea wasp
c) sea bee

How much of a jellyfish's body is made up of water?

a) 99%
b) 80%
c) 65%

(answers on page 32)

DEADLY POISON

Spiny pufferfish

Some creatures have developed some sharp means of defense. The puffer-fish gets its name because it can puff itself up like a balloon: not that scary, until you see how it swells out its spiny, prickly skin. If a hunter is still foolish (or hungry) enough to attack, the puffer has a deadly weapon: poison!

ARMED TO THE TEETH

The poison in a pufferfish is called tetraodontoxin—but puffers aren't the only ones to have it. Two very small, very beautiful types of octopus contain exactly the same poison! These are the blue-ringed octopi. One type lives off the coast of Australia and the other type lives in Indonesia and the Philippines.

Blue-ringed octopus

OCTOPUS NURSERY

What do you call a baby octopus? An octopod!

DISH OF DEATH

The most poisonous of all the puffers is the death puffer. Almost everything about it is horribly poisonous—its heart, liver, guts, bones, and any eggs in its stomach. Its flesh, however, is not (so long as it's been thoroughly cleaned) and the Japanese like to dance with death and eat the fish raw as a delicacy. This dangerous dish is known as fugu. Fugu chefs have to train for at least three years, but even so, there are accidents!

THE POISON TAKES HOLD

If you eat poisonous fugu, you soon know about it. The first signs are a tingly mouth and dizziness. Next, you lose control of your muscles, have fits and find it hard to breathe. There's a 60 per cent chance of being dead within a few hours.

DEADLY OCTOPUS

If a blue-ringed octopus bit you, you could be dead within minutes. The creature carries poison in its saliva and if it nips you with its parrot-like beak, the poison can enter your bloodstream. Worst of all, the bite is painless, so you might not even realise you'd been poisoned—until it was too late.

How many people die of fugu poisoning each year?

a) 5
b) 50
c) 100

Which of these is a Japanese "remedy" for fugu poisoning?

a) pouring boiling water down the victim's throat
b) burying the victim up to their neck in sand
c) making the victim eat shark meat

How big is a blue-ringed octopus?

a) 7.8 inches across
b) 19.6 inches across
c) 196.8 inches across

(answers on page 32)

DEVIL FISH

SEA QUIZ

Why did the ancient Romans make people touch electric rays?

a) as a cure for headaches
b) as a punishment for eating meat on a fast day
c) as a punishment for forgetting your homework

How do electric rays and stingrays reproduce?

a) they fix their egg cases to strands of kelp
b) they give birth to live young
c) the storkray brings them

How big is the biggest electric ray?

a) 1 yard long
b) 2 yards long
c) 3 yards long

(answers on page 32)

The oceans are home to some weird creatures and the kite-shaped rays are one of the strangest of all. Related to the sharks, there are about 400 different kinds of ray, including whip-tailed stingrays, shocking electric rays, and razor-toothed sawfish.

Stingray

WHAT'S IN A NAME?

Electric rays go under many different names, but whether you call them a torpedo ray, a crampfish, or a numbfish the hint is the same— they have the power to shock. In fact, they can send out a bolt of electricity measuring 220 volts.

HOW SHOCKING!

The electric ray gives off enough electricity to light up a lightbulb!

STING IN THE TAIL

The width of a manta ray can range from 9 inches to 78 inches, but they all have one thing in common—their whip-tail. This lethal weapon has poisonous spines and can be lashed so powerfully that it can get stuck in the hull of a wooden boat! Steer clear of large mantas—a whipping from one of them can inject enough poison into your body to kill you.

GO TO THE DEVIL

Manta rays are sometimes nicknamed "devil fish" because of the two pointy fins that look like the devil's horns sticking out of their head. This swift swimmer looks a bit like a UFO—and although it can't fly, it does sometimes heave itself out of the water and splash back down with a big belly-flop!

THEY'RE ELECTRIFYING!

Electric eel

Electric rays are not alone in having the power to shock. Stargazers can do it too, and so can some river creatures, such as the electric eel of South America and the electric catfish of Africa. The catfish's "electric" organ is a simple layer of muscle just under the skin and can send out shocks twice as strong as the electric ray's. The electric eel produces even more powerful shocks that can measure up to 650 volts—that's a lot of electricity!

THAR SHE BLOWS!

Strange creatures don't have the monopoly on what's scary under the sea. Way down deep, Earth itself does things that would fill you with terror, if you could be there to see them. There are gushing vents of scalding water, flows of bubbling lava, and strange, sulphur-eating worms.

BLACK SMOKERS

Where a volcanic crack on the floor of the ocean is spewing out fountains of boiling-hot water, few creatures can survive. These hot spots are called black smokers, and chimneys form around them made from the grains of minerals that shoot out from beneath Earth's crust. One of these minerals is sulphur, which is deadly poisonous to us, but makes a tasty meal for deep-water bacteria.

BACTERIA BEANFEAST

The sulphur-rich bacteria in turn feed glowing shrimp and giant tubeworms. These stripy, red and white worms thrive on the stuff and grow to be as long as buses!

Giant tubeworms

WATER PA-LAVA!

Underwater lava flow

Some underwater volcanoes ooze out lava instead of jets of hot water. The Hawaiian islands were formed millions of years ago as lava piled up—and more islands are being born right now. In the cold ocean currents, the lava moves slowly and sets quickly, forming shapes like billowing pillows.

BIRTH OF AN ISLAND

The most famous volcanic island was born in the 1960s, off the coast of Iceland. Surtsey was named after the Icelandic god of fire, Sutur. It was the first time scientists had witnessed the birth of an island for themselves. Within a few years, seeds had fallen on the new land in seabirds' droppings and plants were beginning to grow.

SEA QUIZ

In which year was the island of Surtsey born?

a) 1960
b) 1963
c) 1969

Where are most of the world's volcanoes?

a) on the ocean floor
b) in Japan
c) in California

What's the name of the submarine that photographs volcanoes in the Mid-Atlantic Ridge?

a) Arturio
b) Ann-Janine
c) Alvin

(answers on page 32)

CAUGHT ON FILM

Many movie-makers have tried to capture the terror of the seas on the silver screen. Some have told tales of fantastical sea beasts, while others have shown real-life horrors, such as man-eating sharks.

JAWS STORY

In the blockbuster film *Jaws* (1975), an island beach resort is terrorized by a bloodthirsty great white shark. Part of the film's success was that the star of the show, the shark, was created by cleverly mixing real footage of great whites with shots of a full-size man-made model. The movie built up to nail-biting suspense as three men headed out to sea and tried to track down the killer.

TERRIFYING TITANS

The 1981 film *Clash of the Titans* took its inspiration from Greek mythology. The hero Perseus had to fight strange monsters on his way to rescue a beautiful princess called Andromeda. The film had some stunning special effects, with monsters recreated using state-of-the-art photography and clay models!

A MONSTER IS BORN

The ocean is so vast that, in our imaginations at least, it could contain almost anything. All sorts of strange monsters have come out of the sea in films, but the most famous of all must be Godzilla. He has helped defend us from alien invaders, starred in his own cartoon show, and was computer-animated in 1998 when Hollywood remade the original film and set it in New York.

FEAR OF SHARKS

Jaws was the most successful horror film of all time and is the main reason why sharks have such a bad reputation today. Though sharks are vicious, shark attacks are rare, but after seeing the film many people thought twice before having a swim in the ocean.

THAT'S DEEP, MAN

The film *20,000 Leagues Under the Sea* was set way deeper than humans have ever explored in real life— 10,000 times deeper than the record-breaking submarine *Trieste* has ever gone.

SEA QUIZ

How much money did the *Jaws* films make?

a) $50,000
b) $5 million
c) more than $500 million

Who directed *Jaws*?

a) Steven Spielberg
b) Clint Eastwood
c) George Lucas

What was Godzilla's child called?

a) Godzuki
b) King Kong
c) Repta

(answers on page 32)

SINGING SIRENS

Mermaids have been around for over 5,000 years and are found in Hindu legends as well as European folklore. Half-woman, half-fish, mermaids are often blamed for luring sailors to their death on the rocks by charming them with their sweet, soulful songs. Countless mermaid movies have been made, usually focusing on the hopeless love between a human man and a mermaid.

Giant squid

MERMAID DISPLAYS

From the 1500s, showmen travelled from town to town offering a bizarre attraction: real mermaids! By the 1800s, mermaids were a craze. Some of the specimens were man-made fakes, others were dried-up fish.

STRETCHY SQUID

Is the giant squid a real-life kraken? This monstrous mollusk is as long as three container trucks!

SAILORS' STORIES

Long before the days of cinema, the story-tellers spun fantastical tales of the sea. Sailors came home with crazy stories of sea dragons, serpents, and human-like creatures, while back in ancient times, writers recorded myths of epic sea journeys featuring magical monsters.

THE KRAKEN AWAKES

The mythical kraken, with its long, squirming tentacles, appears in Scandinavian legends. This sea dragon may have been inspired by sightings of real giant squid.

HYDRA'S HEADS

Greek myths are big on monsters and the hydra must be one of the scariest. This sea dragon had nine heads, even scarier than the monster Scylla that the Greek hero Odysseus had to get past on his epic journey. Scylla had six heads, twelve feet, and a triple row of gnashing teeth!

SEA QUIZ

In what year was the Disney film _The Little Mermaid_ made?

a) 1989
b) 1990
c) 1999

Who killed the Greek sea serpent hydra?

a) Heracles
b) Athene
c) Odysseus

Which creature might be mistaken for a mermaid?

a) manta ray
b) catfish
c) manatee

(answers on page 32)

Index

Quiz answers

- **Page 3** c, 25; b, 34.5 mph; c, 172–252.
- **Page 5** a, b, c, trick question – all three fishes are sharks;
  b, a month or two; c, six times.
- **Page 7** b, more 1 yard; b, 30–100; a, 40.
- **Page 8** a, 47 inches; a, shoaler; b, two.
- **Page 10** c, 59 feet; c, 108.2 feet; c, 2 hours.
- **Page 13** a, saltwater croc; b, their tongue;
  c, pelagic sea snake.
- **Page 14** c, herring gull; b, clownfish; a, off Australia.
- **Page 17** c, 20; a, 13; a, 3.9 inches.

- **Page 18** c, 100; a, scales; a, 1.9 inches.
- **Page 21** c, 119.7 feet; b, sea wasp; a, 99%.
- **Page 23** b, 50; b, burying the victim up to their neck in
  sand; a, 7.8 inches across.
- **Page 24** a, as a cure for headaches; b, they give birth to
  live young; b, 2 yards long.
- **Page 27** b, 1963; a, on the ocean floor; c, Alvin.
- **Page 29** c, more than $500 million; a, Steven Spielberg;
  a, Godzuki.
- **Page 31** a, 1989; a, Heracles; c, manatee.

Acknowledgements

Copyright © 2008 by Saddleback Educational Publishing. All rights reserved. No part of this book may be reproduced in any form or
by any means, electronic or mechanical, including photocopying, recording, or by any information storage and retrieval system
without the written permission of the publisher.

First published in Great Britain by ticktock Publishing Ltd.● Printed in Guangzhou, China 0510/05-84-10

ISBN-10: 1-59905-244-X ISBN-13: 978-1-59905-244-1 eBook: 978-1-60291-605-0

Picture Credits: t = top, b = bottom, c = center, l = left, r=right, OFC = outside front cover, OBC = outside back cover, IFC = inside front cover
Ann Ronan @ Image select; 10/11, 16b. AKG Photo; 2/3, 2b, 4/5b, 8/9,10b, 12b, 18/19, 23b. Fortean Picture Library; IFC, 6/7, 6b, 12/13t, 25, 25/26, 28. Image Select; 20/21t,
20/21. PIX; 27. Planet Earth Pictures; 14/15. Rex Picture; 8b. Telegraph Colour Library; 26. The Kobal Collection; OFC (main pic), 4/5t, 14t, 16/17, 19b, 22/23, 29, 30/31, 31.